ANIMAL ODYSSEYS

BACK FROM THE EDGE: THE AMERICAN BISON

Lynn M. Stone

THE ROURKE CORPORATION, INC.
Vero Beach, FL 32964

Photo Credits:

© Lynn M. Stone: all photos except pages as noted.
© Jerry Hennen: 42.
© Montana Historical Society: 39.
© Kansas State Historical Society: 5, 29, 33, 36, 41.

Library of Congress Cataloging in Publication Data

Stone, Lynn M.
    Back from the edge: the American bison / by Lynn M. Stone.
        p. cm. – (Animal odysseys)
    Includes index.
    Summary: Describes the history and near-extinction of the American bison or buffalo and its preservation today mainly in parks and preserves.
    ISBN 0-86593-101-1
    1. Bison, American – United States – Juvenile literature. 2. Wildlife conservation – United States – Juvenile literature. [1. Bison. 2. Wildlife conservation.] I. Title. II. Series: Stone, Lynn M. Animal odysseys.
QL737.U53S7434 1991
333.95'9–dc20
                          90-38385
                                CIP
                                AC

CONTENTS

1. THE AMAZING BUFFALO 4

2. NOMADS OF THE PLAINS 14

3. PREDATORS, PREY, AND PRAIRIES 17

4. BEFORE BUFFALO BILL 23

5. THE INDIANS' BUFFALO 28

6. THE TRAIL OF BONES 32

7. BACK FROM THE EDGE 40

   GLOSSARY 46

   INDEX 47

   WHERE TO SEE BISON 48

1
THE AMAZING BUFFALO

It's hard to lose something that weighs a ton, like a bull buffalo. Losing several million buffalo is even more difficult. But the world almost lost the American bison, every last one of them.

The bison, better known as the buffalo, is the biggest land animal in North America. A bull may be six feet tall and measure nine feet from its bearded chin to its short tail. Even a female, or cow, buffalo may weigh 1,300 pounds.

One by one, these great, shaggy creatures were shot almost out of existence. Their size made them easy targets, and buffalo were so plentiful that few people realized they were being killed much faster than they could replace themselves.

The sad story of the buffalo's decline tells us about human greed and stupidity. It tells us about the gross mistreatment not only of buffalo but also of the Indians who depended upon them. In turn, the heartening story

Above:

Thousands of buffalo hides lie stacked in Dodge City, Kansas, in 1874.

of the bison's comeback tells us something about conservation and how a few concerned people managed to save a species from **extinction**. But the bittersweet **odyssey** of the American bison back from the very brink of disaster begins with this amazing animal itself.

No one claims the bison is beautiful, yet an adult bull is an unquestionably impressive animal with a shoulder hump like New Hampshire's Mount Washington. The hump is one of the characteristics that separates the American bison and its European cousin, the European bison or wisent, from the true buffalo of Asia and Africa. The African and Asian buffalo, which have long, widespread horns, don't have the bison's shoulder

5

hump. Along with the distinctive hump, a bison bull wears a long beard and woolly "cape," or robe, over its shoulders. It has a pair of short, sharp upswept horns, split hooves, a massive head, a deep chest, and narrow hindquarters.

The most exciting time to watch a buffalo bull is in the late summer or early fall. This time of year is the mating season, or **rut**, when bulls think they are in love with every buffalo cow that comes near. During the rut a bull's nature changes from generally easy-going to explosive. Bulls are always unpredictable creatures; bison

Above:
The adult American bison bull is the largest land animal in North America.

6

Right:
The African buffalo has broad, sweeping horns and lacks the bison's hump, shaggy coat, and beard.

bulls have gored scores of careless people, including farmers who have raised them as pets. The rut, however, makes a buffalo bull particularly dangerous to anyone or anything that crosses his path.

The rut is the season of fury. Bulls paw the earth, butt heads, and constantly snort and bellow. Their hoarse, rumbling bellows carry well over a mile in the wind. Their bloodshot eyes roll, and their mouths are lathered with drool.

The head-butting can be quite serious. Although the bulls would rather attend their cows than fight, they

Below:
On a frosty morning, two buffalo bulls battle head-to-head.

8

Right:
A buffalo bull only looks sleepy and slow; he can run 35 miles per hour.

sometimes fight anyway. They normally slam head against head, so their thick skulls and hair absorb most of the shock. When one bull catches another's flank, he can open a frightful wound. Occasionally one bull gores another to death.

A bull's need to show his power over other buffalo is extremely strong. When his anger rises, he may take on a rival bull or even lunge with a sweep of his horns at a cow.

Grazing or peacefully chewing their **cuds**, buffalo look like dark, shaggy, overstuffed cows. In fact, they are closely related to cows. Cows, wild cattle, buffalo, bison, and other hoofed, cud-chewing mammals make up the group scientists call **bovids**. But more than one person has approached bison on foot, only to learn that they are far quicker and more nimble than cows. A buffalo can lumber up to 35 miles per hour, which is much faster than a person can run flat-out. A newspaper in Illinois once printed a photo of a bison bull in a fenced pasture. As a warning to would-be trespassers, the caption under the photo read, "Can you run across this pasture in 10 seconds? The bull can."

The buffalo's eyes are nearsighted; it can see nearby things more clearly than distant objects. It makes up for faulty vision with keen senses of smell and hearing. When danger threatens, a buffalo can race across open

Below:
A buffalo bull rolls in a dust wallow to rid himself of itches and pesky insects.

land or gallop up rocky slopes. It can turn quickly, swim well, and, it is said, outmaneuver a dog.

Despite its unpredictability and ability to move quickly, a buffalo is usually content to graze, chew its cud, and occasionally roll in a dirt wallow. Rolling is a favorite pastime. Buffalo roll in clouds of dust to rid themselves of itches, insects, and loose hair.

Like most bovids, the buffalo has a strong attachment to being with others of its own kind. Except for old bulls, buffalo live in herds. Adult bulls herd together, while young bulls, cows, and calves travel in other herds. When the rut begins, the big bulls rejoin the cows and calves.

Buffalo herds range from as small as 10 or 12 animals to as large as 500. The great herds that the pioneers described, some of them seemingly endless in number, were apparently made up of many smaller herds joined together for seasonal journeys.

Most buffalo cows at the age of two or three produce calves. Twins are rare, and a cow usually has only two calves every three years. Calves are born in the spring.

The reddish-brown calf weighs about 50 pounds. It stands, nurses, and may even run within five minutes after birth. With luck, it can live to be 25 or 30 years old.

American bison all belong to the same **species**, or kind, scientifically known as *Bison bison.* Nevertheless, the bison of wooded northern Canada and the bison of the plains are somewhat different in appearance. The wood buffalo, as the northern animals are called, tend to be larger and darker than the plains buffalo. Unlike the wood buffalo, plains buffalo have a ruff of hair, or "chaps," on the back of their front legs. The European bison is similar in size, structure, and appearance to its American cousins.

2 NOMADS OF THE PLAINS

Part of the reason for the American bison's rapid disappearance was its choice of home, or **habitat**. Bison were originally found over much of North America, but they were most abundant on the American grasslands of the central West. Some of that land became extremely valuable for homesteading, and because it was generally open, buffalo were easy to spot, track, and shoot.

Before white Europeans began settling North America, beginning with the Spanish in the early 1500s, bison lived anywhere from northern Canada south to Mexico and northern Florida. They ranged east to New York and the Carolinas and west into the foothills of the Rockies, the mountain passes of Oregon and Washington, and into northwestern Canada.

Buffalo moved from one place to another often, but not necessarily in a predictable way. They were **nomads**, true wanderers, but they didn't have true, long-distance **migrations**. In fact, bison probably didn't move more than 300 or 400 miles from a starting point.

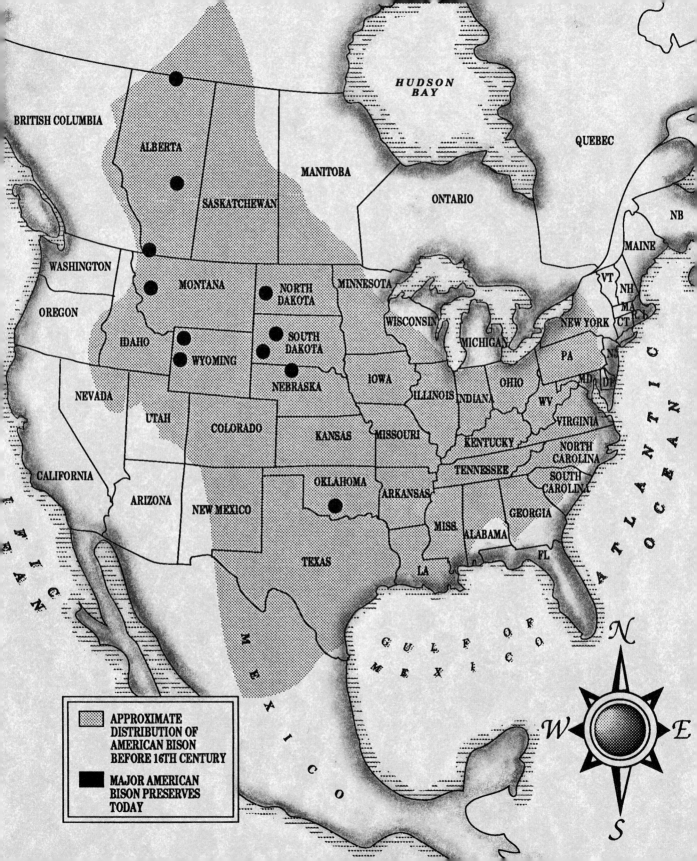

Animals that migrate, such as geese, follow pre-dictable seasonal schedules and routes for their journeys. Bison travels were less predictable. Generally, the great herds of buffalo probably did move southward in the winter and northward in the spring, but not over great distances. Even today, the free-ranging wood buffalo of northern Alberta, Canada, undertake a short annual journey. Each November they trek up to 170 miles from wooded hills to the relative shelter of the Peace River valley. In May they return to the woods. The Yellowstone National Park bison also engage in seasonal movements from high country to low, protected valleys and back.

Plains bison moved as they ate up grass in one place and looked for more. They were also driven to find water, to escape exceptionally hot or harsh weather, and to avoid swarms of insects. Their travels took them in many directions and at different times of year. One year's travels did not duplicate the previous year's.

3
PREDATORS, PREY, AND PRAIRIES

The grasslands of the central West were the perfect home for American bison. Most of a bison's diet is grass, and the rolling plains, carpeted in buffalo grass and other grass species, were a banquet table for the once-great herds. The living was easiest in the late spring when the new green sprouts flourished. Later in the summer, insects, hot weather, and drought sometimes forced the buffalo to wander in search of better food and adequate water.

When bitter weather surprised buffalo in the winter, they were well-equipped to tough it out. They had endurance to move on and seek shelter, and they had heavy winter coats to protect them against all but the harshest cold and snows. Normally, they were able to feed on grass by using their heads to sweep away snow.

The bison took most of their energy and nourishment from eating the **prairie** grasses, but they also gave something back. Their droppings fertilized the prairie,

17

replacing **nutrients**. Their woolly coats snatched grass seeds – quite by accident, of course – in one place and released them elsewhere. In this way, the moving herds helped plant the wild grasses upon which they and other grass-eating animals depended.

The buffalo may have also helped keep the grasslands from being invaded in some areas by woodland. Trampling, and the bulls' habit of horning and butting trees, undoubtedly destroyed many small trees that might otherwise have survived and crowded out plots of grass.

Above:
Protected by heavy coats, buffalo are rarely bothered by winter snows.

18

Right:
A buffalo cow with a mouthful of prairie grass.

19

Buffalo wallows were useful to many prairie animals. The wallows were shallow basins which trapped rain water. As temporary ponds, they provided water, nesting, and even short-lived vegetation for a variety of creatures.

Bison lived side-by-side with most of the prairie animals. The other plant eaters, or **herbivores**, were no threat to the buffalo, nor were the buffalo any real threat to them. Occasionally, it is true, a buffalo would drive an elk, mule deer, or pronghorn antelope from its neighborhood. Prairie dogs were often sent scurrying for the underground safety of their burrows as the buffalo herds trampled through their towns and rolled in their dirt mounds.

The prairie community of the western plains today is much different than the one that existed 120 or 150 years ago. Pronghorn antelope, mule deer, and prairie dogs are still there in fair numbers. However, much of the original, wild grassland cover has been plowed, grazed, or reseeded with foreign grasses. The plains elk and buffalo are gone. And the **predators** – wolves, grizzlies, and other hunting animals that used to sharpen their teeth on the big herbivores – are gone too.

Now buffalo live on the prairies only in controlled situations. Cattle guards, fences, and wildlife managers keep the buffalo within certain limits, both in terms of the space that they occupy and the size of their herds. Formerly, buffalo were probably important sources of

Above:
Pronghorns share the prairies with bison, prairie dogs, and other plant eaters.

prey to prairie wolves and grizzly bears. With wolves and plains grizzlies no more than memories, the plains buffalo don't have any predators.

Buffalo and grizzlies still live together in Yellowstone National Park, which is a mix of prairie, wetlands, and woods. Grizzlies feed on winter-killed buffalo, as do coyotes, but these grizzlies rarely kill buffalo. When wolves are reintroduced to Yellowstone National Park, they will probably live largely on elk. They may also kill young or injured bison, as their forefathers did.

In northern Canada, the wood buffalo are truly wild animals. They are often hunted by wolves, which

specialize in taking old, young, sick, or injured victims. Healthy adult buffalo show little concern over wolves.

In the old days, many buffalo drowned after recklessly plunging into fast, rain-swollen rivers. Others died in blizzards, from lightning strikes, or in mad stampedes over cliffs. Most of the buffalo that charged over cliffs were probably being chased by Indians.

Indians killed buffalo by the hundreds, but the cause of the buffalo's fall was not the American Indian. Rather, it was the result of westward expansion by a young, land-hungry America.

Above:
Although no longer found on the plains, wolves still hunt buffalo in northern Canada.

4 BEFORE BUFFALO BILL

William Frederick Cody, better know as Buffalo Bill, claimed to have killed 4,280 buffalo during a 17-month period in 1867-68. But Cody can't take all the credit, or the blame, for nearly wiping out the American bison, or buffalo, as a species. When Cody's Springfield rifle was smoking on the buffalo plains, there were a few *million* buffalo. Cody's activities didn't make much of an impact on the buffalo population as a whole.

The trouble was, Cody had plenty of company. For several years, thousands of buffalo hunters shot as many buffalo as they could find. The thousands of buffalo that each killed began to add up. The sprawling herds, which at one time had darkened the plains and prairies of the American West, began to shrink. In 1883 the last big herd was slaughtered by hunters. The American bison was suddenly on the brink of extinction. Incredibly, an animal that had existed in the millions was being killed in such numbers that it was in danger of disappearing altogether. It had arrived at this point in just a few years.

Today it is difficult for us to imagine how big the great herds once were. Of course, it is almost as hard to imagine the vast, roadless plains where most of the buffalo lived. The plains are still there, but they have farms, fences, roads, and cities. It is no wonder that we can't picture huge, milling herds of thousands upon thousands of 1,500-pound animals in such a setting. The settlers, understandably, couldn't picture their new towns and farms with wild buffalo herds either.

Buffalo Bill Cody earned his nickname for killing buffalo. But he was just a droplet in a tidal wave of westward settlement. It was the whole process of settlement, not the marksmanship of Buffalo Bill or any of the thousands of other buffalo hunters, that doomed the great herds. The hunters were merely products of the conditions.

No one will ever know how many millions of buffalo once roamed through North America from almost one edge to the other. We do know that before the Europeans began to establish posts in North America, prior to the sixteenth century, the numbers were staggering. Even as late as the first half of the nineteenth century, when Buffalo Bill Cody was born, the number of buffalo must have been almost beyond imagination.

We can only guess at how many buffalo there once were. Today we can count large animals from the air.

Right:
Buffalo herds today are small when compared with the vast herds that darkened the plains.

But when buffalo lived in large numbers as wild animals, there was no way to count them all. In fact, there was no way to count even a large herd.

The journals of the western settlers and explorers often mention the herds of buffalo. Many of these plains people wished they could tell their readers and the people "back east" how many buffalo they had seen. They were amazed at the size of the herds, but they were somewhat frustrated by their inability to count the animals. No one, however, then or now, can count from ground level individual animals in a herd that sprawls past his field of view.

The estimates of buffalo numbers at their peak range from 30 million to 75 million. Based on what scientists now think was once good buffalo land, the lower estimates are probably more accurate. Whatever the number actually was, it is likely that no other large wild animal anywhere ever reached the abundance of the American bison.

By today's standards, the hundreds of thousands of wild caribou in Canada and Alaska represent a huge population. More than 1 million wildebeest in Africa represent the greatest number of any one kind of wild, four-legged herd animals on Earth. Yet neither the caribou nor the wildebeest herds compare in number to the herds of American bison that existed before Buffalo Bill and the westward migration of Americans.

Having no way to count the bison, the pioneers sometimes measured the herds in time and distance. Colonel Richard Dodge watched a herd of buffalo travel past his observation post in the early 1800s. Dodge said that the herd was 25 miles wide and it took five days to pass. William Street, a pioneer in northwestern Kansas, described a buffalo herd he saw in 1869. "How many buffaloes were in that herd?" he wrote. "And the answer no one could tell. The herd was not less than 20 miles in width – we never saw the other side – at least 60 miles in length, maybe much longer; two counties of buffaloes! There might have been 100,000 or 1,000,000, or 100,000,000. I don't know."

The days of the great herds, however, were coming to an end faster than anyone, Indian or white, could imagine.

5
THE INDIANS' BUFFALO

Before the settlement of the West, the Indians of the plains and prairies lived comfortably with the great herds of buffalo. The number of buffalo exceeded the number of Indians many times over. No matter how many buffalo the Kiowa, Comanche, Sioux, Arapaho, Blackfeet, Pawnee, Cheyenne, and other tribes killed, there were always more. The Indians made no dent in the buffalo population. Nor did they wish to. The Indians needed the buffalo, and more importantly they *knew* they needed the buffalo. Unlike the white settlers who came west, the Indians didn't waste the animals they killed, and they did not kill what they could not use. The Indians considered the buffalo to be unfailingly wise and powerful. Buffalo bulls were held in exceptionally high regard. The great Sioux warrior and medicine man Sitting Bull was named for the animal.

The lifestyles of many Plains Indians were thoroughly linked to the buffalo. When the pioneers began to thread westward in the early 1800s, at least two dozen

Above:

The lifestyles of Plains Indians depended upon the availability of bison.

Indian tribes depended on the buffalo for part or nearly all of their needs. Much of what glass, steel, plastic, oil, and timber provides for modern man, the buffalo provided for the Indians. One plainsman observed that, for the Indians, buffalo were "meat, drink, shoes, house, fire vessels, and. . .whole substance." That wasn't far from the truth.

It is sometimes said that we can use all of a pig except its squeal. The Indians used all of a buffalo except its bellow. The big difference in modern Americans' use of hogs and the Indians' use of bison is that we don't depend on hogs; we can take them or leave them. The Indians needed buffalo, and when the U.S. government began to understand that, both the Indians and the buffalo were pushed quickly toward disaster.

Buffalo meat was a major source of food for the Plains Indians, and buffalo blood and juices were occasional beverages. The Indians had multiple non-food uses for the bison too. Indians used buffalo skins for saddles, clothing, movable teepees, ropes, and shields. They made glue from buffalo hooves. The ligaments in the animals' legs became bowstrings and twine. Buffalo bones were used for weapons and for such tools as hoes. Buffalo skulls were sometimes saved for their "great medicine." The buffalo's woolly hair was used to pad saddles, fill leather-covered balls, and to cushion beds and back rests. Beards were used for ornaments. The buffalo's tail could be a whip, fly swatter, or decoration. Horns were modeled into spoons, cups, arrowheads, and bowls. From other parts of the buffalo, the Indians made rattles, stirrup covers, water bags, bow wrapping, paint, dice, and paint brushes. Even buffalo droppings, or chips, were valuable as fuel and markers. When dry, buffalo chips burned fiercely and with a minimum of smoke. Piled atop each other, they stood out on flat or rolling ground.

Buffalo were so important that they influenced all phases of Indian life. Some plains tribes became nomads, just like the wandering buffalo they sought to follow. The Indians' religion and ideas about the Earth were closely allied with the buffalo and their yearly movements.

In the days before they had rifles, the Indians killed buffalo largely with bows and arrows or spears. They also killed buffalo by stampeding them over cliffs, which became know as "buffalo jumps."

For about 10,000 years American Indians coexisted with buffalo. They simply took from buffalo stocks what they needed. During that 10,000 years, the buffalo suffered no lasting effects from the Indians, and the Indians, knowing buffalo were their lifeblood, held the animals in great respect. When Europeans began to descend on the plains and prairies in ever greater numbers, they viewed the Indian and the buffalo alike. Both were in the way of settlement. Buffalo were not as simple to herd as cattle, and as for the Indians – they could be downright dangerous, especially when their land and buffalo were being swallowed up by these newcomers.

6
THE TRAIL
OF BONES

By late 1883 nothing was left of the great buffalo herds except their bones. Picked clean by wolves, coyotes, magpies, and armies of insects, buffalo bones littered the plains. Eventually many of them were picked up and ground into fertilizer.

In the autumn of 1883, the buffalo hunters fanned across the northern plains and waited, as they had in previous years. The aspen leaves yellowed and the prairie grasses turned bronze. Surely the herds would be trekking south into the shortgrass plains from Canada. But the buffalo did not come that fall or ever again. There were none. The millions of rumbling buffalo that had once seemed almost as plentiful as the shoots of prairie grass no longer existed. Their dust wallows were empty, and their trails were strewn with their bones.

The buffalo hadn't disappeared entirely. A few – only 20, some say – survived in the new Yellowstone National Park that straddled northwestern Wyoming and southwestern Montana. Some wood buffalo still lived

Right:
The buffalo industry of the nineteenth century developed a market for bones (left, in stacks) as well as for hides and flesh.

in remote northern Canada. Several dozen more buffalo lived in private farm herds. But for all practical purposes, the wild buffalo had vanished, and the species was a hair's breadth from extinction.

The buffalo, of course, had not disappeared overnight, although it seemed that way to the buffalo hunters in the fall of 1883. The buffalo population actually began to tumble slowly as soon as the continent was settled by Spanish, French, and English **colonists**. By 1800, shortly after the American Revolution, buffalo were nearly gone everywhere east of the Mississippi River. That caused no great concern. Buffalo had never been plentiful east of the big, muddy river, and farmers didn't want buffalo tearing up their plots and fences anyway.

By 1830 the westward migration of settlers from the East had begun in earnest. In the wake of those early settlers, there remained millions of buffalo, but not as many millions as there had been.

In the years that followed, the wagon trains heading west became longer. Thousands of settlers poured into the western territories. After the Civil War ended in 1865, the rush of settlers to the West came faster than a prairie fire.

The American West was largely Indian territory, or at least the Indians thought so. The Indians, who depended upon the buffalo and other wild game, were worried by the flood of white settlers. Naturally, they were also angered at having to share traditional hunting lands with outsiders who killed for sport and wandered wherever they pleased.

The conflicts between the interests of the Indians and whites led to several decades of on-again, off-again warfare. Treaties were made and broken. For nearly 20 years, beginning in the late 1860s, large numbers of U.S. Army troops – the pony soldiers of the U.S. Cavalry – were stationed on the plains to protect settlers, wagon trains, railroad crews, and prospectors. They were also there to put Indians onto **reservations**, by force if necessary.

The presence of the soldiers and their long rifles eventually forced most of the Plains Indians off their traditional hunting grounds. General George Armstrong Custer's "last stand" resulted in the death of 265 American soldiers in a single day in June, 1876, but it was the Indians who suffered most over the years. Thousands of Indians were killed in the years of bloodshed. The ones who survived war, starvation, and disease were placed on reservations.

General Phil Sheridan helped defeat the Plains Indians. Afterward, Sheridan observed, "We took away their country, and their means of support, broke up their mode of living, their habits of life, introduced disease and decay among them, and it was for this and against this that they made war. Could anyone expect less?"

Central to this warfare between the whites and the Indians was the buffalo. After all, the means of support that Sheridan talked about was none other than the buffalo.

Right:
Memorial markers rise from the hills in Montana where General George Custer and 264 fellow troopers were killed by Indians on June 25, 1876.

By 1870, about 15 years before the wars with the Indians ended, buffalo hunting had become the major industry of the plains. Buffalo robes (the shoulder capes), tongues, dried meat, and leather were being shipped by train back to the East. Train loads, one after another, were sent eastward. The Indians had good reason to dread the future. Posts were set up just to market buffalo products.

The U.S. Army was not in the buffalo-hunting business. But it encouraged the buffalo hunters and made sure they had plenty of free ammunition. It was apparent that if the buffalo were eliminated, the threat of hostile Indians would also be eliminated. As the 1870s melted away, the Plains Indians faced two ugly choices: starvation or reservation. On the reservations, they knew, the government would at least feed them. Gradually, the

Left:
The Kansas Pacific Rail road offered "sportsmen" a chance to shoot buffalo from its trains.

strategy worked. The Indians retreated to reservations to avoid starving to death.

The government's efforts to rid the plains of Indians was one reason for the unchecked slaughter of buffalo. The demand for buffalo products was another. The arrival of the railroad was a third. Starting in the late 1860s, railroads like the Union Pacific and Kansas Pacific expanded westward. The railroads hired buffalo hunters, including Buffalo Bill Cody, to supply their construction gangs with meat. Later, as the railways were finished, "sportsmen" were offered a chance to shoot buffalo from the train car windows. A railroad conductor in the 1870s recalled that a man could have hiked along 100 miles of railroad track without ever stepping off the carcasses of buffalo.

Reasons for some of the slaughter were understandable. Settlers were terrified of Indians, and the government was under pressure to remove the threat. Buffalo products were in demand, and there seemed to be an endless herd of buffalo. In addition, ranchers had no use for buffalo; these wild cattle competed with their **domestic** cattle and sheep for grass.

If the reasons for the mass destruction of buffalo were understandable, they weren't necessarily just. Along with the killing came a tremendous amount of waste. Until 1872 there was no means of refrigeration for sending tons of meat eastward. Buffalo meat that wasn't carefully dried or served immediately rotted on the prairie. Since the early refrigeration on train cars wasn't very effective, much of the waste continued.

Two thousand-pound buffalo bulls were sometimes shot just for their four-pound tongues, which were said to be the most tasty part of the animal. The loss of meat and hides was incredible. As early as 1848, the American

Fur Company shipped 110,000 buffalo hides to St. Louis. For every hide that was shipped, another four or five were left to rot. ———

Many sportsmen wanted to shoot a buffalo. Killing buffalo had become a popular sport for visitors to the plains but it was as sporting as shooting fish in a tank. Buffalo would sometimes panic and bolt if fired upon, but at other times herd members would stand around while gunners dropped them one by one. When they had a standing herd, professional shooters could kill 250 buffalo in a day. One man killed 120 bison in less than an hour on a day in 1872.

Meanwhile, skinners stripped the meat and hides. A skillful skinner could dress a carcass in five minutes. Sometimes skinners weren't necessary. The buffalo were shot by people who just wanted to watch them fall dead.

Left: *Bellowing in the dust of its wallow, a buffalo bull extends the four-pound tongue for which thousands of its ancestors were killed.*

Right:
In one of the last hunts of free, wild buffalo, skinners in northern Montana dress a bull in January, 1882.

The herds on the southern plains were gone by 1874. The hunters swept next onto the northern plains. In 1882, over 5,000 hunters and skinners were in Montana and the Dakota Territory, but the hunting wasn't very good. That year the Northern Pacific Railroad shipped just 200,000 hides to the East. Early in 1883 hunters wiped out several small herds and destroyed a herd of 10,000, the last big herd of wild bison in North America. The buffalo industry was left with only bones to process.

In 1887, hunters for the American Museum of Natural History in New York spent three months looking for wild buffalo. They found none. If they *had* found a bison and it had been the last American bison on Earth, the hunters, sad to say, would have killed it. They were looking for a specimen to stuff and display. The notion of wildlife protection – keeping species alive – had few champions in 1887.

7

BACK FROM THE EDGE

When the first colonists settled in North America, they found an abundance of wild animals. They often killed more animals than they needed. The colonists believed that the land and everything on it was theirs to do with as they saw fit. The Indians believed the opposite: that they were caretakers of the land and should take only what they needed.

The idea that government and laws should limit what they killed was out of the question for American settlers. It should not be surprising, then, that there was no general outrage about the buffalo slaughter. A few people were saddened, however. The famous American artist and **naturalist** John James Audubon wrote in 1843 that, "like the **great auk**, before many years the buffalo will vanish. Surely this should not be permitted?" General Hazen, commander at Fort Hays, Kansas, also noted the killing, which he called "this wicked waste, both of the lives of God's creatures and the valuable food they furnish."

Right:

A guide and his wealthy client shoot buffalo in this drawing, which was entitled "Sport on the Plains" and published by Harpers Weekly in 1874.

In Kansas, a Topeka newspaper published in June, 1872, cautioned that the bison was "rapidly. . .disappearing from western plains." Disgusted, another writer observed, "I see no more sport in shooting a buffalo than in shooting an ox."

Action to save the buffalo bordered on the comical. Idaho passed a law in 1864 to protect buffalo during the calving season, but the mountains and forests of Idaho had very few buffalo. It was almost like Florida acting to protect polar bears. Protective laws were eventually enacted by New Mexico (1880), Nebraska (1875), and the Dakota Territory (1883) – after the buffalo had vanished from those regions.

As early as 1871, members of Congress debated the buffalo slaughter. In 1874 Congress passed a law to protect buffalo cows. However, President Ulysses Grant's Secretary of Interior, Columbus Delano, said, "I would not seriously regret the total disappearance of the buffalo from our western prairies, in its effect upon the Indians." Delano, advising the president not to approve the law, added that the sooner the buffalo were gone, the sooner the Indians would have to farm. Everyone, Grant included, knew that until the buffalo were cleared out, many Indians would never submit to the government's reservation policy. President Grant **vetoed** the law. The slaughter continued until the last wild buffalo in the United States were those tucked away in the wilds of Yellowstone National Park.

Yellowstone was supposed to be a haven, off-limits to hunting. In the early days of the park, however, Congress didn't make any money available to enforce park laws, such as they were. **Poachers**, people who hunt against the law, picked away at the Yellowstone herd.

Left:
By 1884, the last wild buffalo in the United States lived in a small band in the wilds of Yellowstone National Park.

Right:
In the twentieth century, the United States government established herds of buffalo in several parks, including Wind Cave National Park in South Dakota, shown here.

When a poacher was caught in 1894 and then released because of a loophole in the law, the press carried the story. Angered, the public finally rallied to the buffalo's defense. To protect the Yellowstone buffalo, Congress soon passed a law that it would stand behind. Gradually the Yellowstone herd began to increase.

In 1905 a small group of individuals formed the American Bison Society. That group and the New York Zoological Society called for bison herds to be established on a few select public lands. With President Theodore R. Roosevelt's help, the government acted. Herds were established at Wichita Mountains National Wildlife Refuge in Oklahoma (1907), the National Bison Range in Montana (1908), and Fort Niobrara National Wildlife Refuge in Nebraska (1913). The buffalo was on its journey back.

In 1905, the federal government had fewer than 100 buffalo, about 50 of them in Yellowstone. Over 500 lived on ranches owned by people who had built their own little herds. The government stocked the new refuges with bison from the private herds.

Canada had lost most of her bison, too. Perhaps only 250 were left when they were put under the protection of the Royal Canadian Mounted Police in 1893. In 1922 Canada established the magnificent Wood Buffalo National Park, 11 million acres of grassy plains, swamp, and forest. The park herd now numbers 15,000.

Yellowstone's herd today contains about 2,000 buffalo. Within the confines of the huge national park the bison can wander as they please.

Elsewhere in the United States and Canada, a total of about 75,000 buffalo live in several national, state, and provincial parks and in dozens of private herds. They have stepped far back from the brink of extinction.

Below:
Today over 2,000 American bison live within the broad, wild confines of Yellowstone National Park.

In 1832, plains artist George Catlin watched as the nation began to creep westward. "The buffaloes' doom is sealed," he said, and Catlin was nearly correct. We count buffalo now in herds of dozens and hundreds, not in millions. But if we haven't kept these great, shaggy creatures around on a grand scale, at least we have kept them around. It would have been a horrible mistake to lose them entirely and never see the prairie as naturalist Aldo Leopold said it should be seen – "under the bellies of the buffalo."

bovid – the family of large, hoofed, plant-eating mammals with four-chambered stomachs

colonist – one who settles new country

cud – food that has been only partially chewed and digested when brought up from a bovid animal's stomach for more thorough chewing

domestic – an animal tamed, raised, and modified by man over a long period of time

extinction – the state of no longer existing

great auk – a flightless seabird of the North Atlantic coast that became extinct in 1844

habitat – a plant or animal's immediate surroundings; its specific, preferred location within the environment

herbivore – a plant eating animal

migration – a predictable and seasonal movement from one location to another some distance away

naturalist – a student of nature

nomad – a wanderer

nutrient – something that furnishes nourishment

odyssey – a long journey

poacher – one who hunts against the law

prairie – the land of midwestern and western North America dominated by wild grasses and other non-woody plants; native grassland

predator – an animal that kills and feeds on other animals

prey – an animal hunted for food by another animal

reservation – a tract of public land set aside for Indians

rut – the mating season, particularly of horned and antlered animals

species – a group of plants or animals whose members reproduce naturally only with other plants or animals of the same group; a particular kind of plant or animal such as a *red* fox

veto – to use one's authority to cancel a law

INDEX

Numbers in boldface type refer to photo and illustration pages.

American Bison Society 44
American Revolution 33
Army, U.S. 34, 36
Audubon, John James 40
bears, grizzly 20, 21
bison, European 5, 13
bones 30, 32, **33**, **39**
bovids 10, 12
buffalo
    African 5, **7**
    Asian 5
    bull 4, 5, **6**, 7, **8**, **9**, 10, **11**, 12, 28, 37, **38**, **39**, 48
    cow 4, 6, 8, 10, 12, 13, **19**, 41
    plains 13, 16, 21
    wood 13, 16, 21, 32
Buffalo Bill, *See* Cody, William Frederick
buffalo jumps 31
calf, buffalo **12**, 13
caribou 26
Catlin, George 45
cattle 10, 31, 37
Cavalry, U.S. 34
chips, buffalo 30, 31
Civil War 34
coats 17, **18**
Cody, William Frederick 23, 24, 37
Congress, U.S. 41, 42, 43
coyotes 21, 32
cud 10, 11
Custer, Gen. George Armstrong 34, **35**
deer, mule 20
Delano, Columbus 41, 42
diet 17
Dodge, Colonel Richard 27
elk 20
Europeans 14, 24, 31
extinction 5, 23, 33, 44
Fort Niobrara National Wildlife Refuge 44, 48
Grant, President Ulysses 41, 42
grass 16, 17, 18, 20, 32, 37
habitat 14
hair 10, 13, 30
Hazen, General 40
herds, buffalo 12, 13, 16, 17, 18, 20, 23, 24, **25**, 26, 27, 28, 32, 33, 39, **43**, 44, 45, 48
hides, buffalo **5**, **33**, 37, 38, 39, *See also* skins, buffalo

hooves 6, 30
horns 5, 6, 10, 30
hump, shoulder 5, 6
hunters, buffalo 23, 24, 32, 33, **36**, 37, 39, **41**
Indians 4, 22, 28, **29**, 30, 31, 34, 35, 36, 37, 40, 42
laws 40, 41, 42
Leopold, Aldo 45
mating season 6, 48, *See also* rut
meat 29, 30, 35, 37, 38
migration 14
    map **15**
National Bison Range 44
New York Zoological Society 44
poachers 42, 43
population 23, 26
prairie 17, 28, 31, 37, 42, 45
prairie dogs 20
pronghorn 20, **21**
railroad 36
    Kansas Pacific **36**
    Northern Pacific 39
    Union Pacific 36
reservations, Indian 34, 36
Roosevelt, Pres. Theodore R. 44
rut 6, 7, 8, 12, *See also* mating season
senses 10
sheep 37
Sheridan, Gen. Phil 35
Sioux 28
Sitting Bull 28
size 4, 13
skinner 38, 39
skins, buffalo 30, *See also* hides, buffalo
stampedes 22, 31
Street, William 27
tongues 35, 37, **38**
trees 18
wallow **11**, 20, 32, **38**
Wichita Mountains National Wildlife Refuge 44
wildebeest 26
Wind Cave National Park **43**
wisent 5
wolves 20, 21, **22**, 32
Wood Buffalo National Park 44
Yellowstone National Park 16, 21, 32, **42**, 44, **45**

Truly wild, free-roaming buffalo exist in few places. One of these places – perhaps the only place, really – is Wood Buffalo National Park in Canada's Northwest Territories. Unfortunately for would-be buffalo watchers, Wood Buffalo National Park is just slightly less remote than the moon. For most buffalo watchers, Yellowstone National Park is a much better alternative. Yellowstone's buffalo are free-roaming, too, at least within the confines of the huge park.

Generally, buffalo herds are kept in fenced preserves. Many of these are expansive and scenic. You may not even notice the fences and the cattle grates on the roads. All of these big, picturesque preserves are located on traditional bison range where the ancestors of today's buffalo once trod without the inconvenience of fencing.

Bison are generally fearless, and people often approach them much too closely. Always treat bison with extreme caution. Despite their enormous size, they are nimble and quick – and quite unpredictable. A buffalo bull during the late summer mating season is a particularly dangerous animal.

Bison Sites

Badlands National Park, SD
Custer State Park, SD
Elk Island National Park, Alberta
Fort Niobrara National Wildlife Refuge, Valentine, NE
Grand Teton National Park, WY
National Bison Range, Moiese, MT
Theodore Roosevelt National Park, ND
Waterton Lakes National Park, Alberta
Wichita Mountains National Wildlife Refuge, Cache, OK
Wind Cave National Park, SD
Yellowstone National Park, WY

Ed. Note: Sites listed here do not represent *all* the places where American bison may be observed. They do represent sites that are reliable and have relatively easy access.